flipped eye publishing

A Day of Presence

simple words, rendered sublime

A Day of Presence
flipped eye publishing
www.flippedeye.net

First Edition
Copyright © Truth Thomas, 2008
Cover Image: *Y'all Ain't Got No Power*, © Thomas Sayers Ellis, 2007
Cover Design © flipped eye publishing, 2008

Enduring thanks to the editors of the following publications in which versions of these poems have appeared:

Fingernails Across the Chalkboard: Poetry and Prose on HIV/AIDS from the Black Diaspora - *Visiting Hours are Over*
Quiddity Literary Journal - *Dreamgirl, The Power of a Teenage Brain*
The Progressive - *There is No Fried Chicken in Heaven*
Party of Black (pamphlet) - *A Time to Kiss, There is No Fried Chicken in Heaven*
The Ringing Ear: Black Poets Lean South: Cave Canem Anthology - *I Love it When You Call Me Big Country*
Warpland Literary Journal - *Blind Horse*
Alehouse - *Marley: Wailing for Peace, BET*

ISBN-10: 0-9818584-0-6
ISBN-13: 978-0-9818584-0-1

A Day of Presence

Truth Thomas
2008

Gratitude

To God, Mom, Cherry, Soweto, Randall, Tara Betts, Derrick Weston Brown, Josue Cedeno, Stephan Delbos, Joel Dias-Porter (aka DJ Renegade), Chard deNiord, Thomas Sayers Ellis, Jaime "Shaggy" Flores, Cherryl Floyd-Miller, Asha French, Jeff Friedman, Carol Frost, Ross Gay, Jacqueline Gens, Regie O'Hare Gibson, Reverend Darrell S. Greene, Judith Hall, Chanell Harris, M. Ayodele Heath, Melanie Henderson, Howard County Poetry and Literary Society, Howard University, M. L. Hunter, Fred Joiner, Ilya Kaminsky, Alan King, Ruth Ellen Kocher, Maxine Kumin, Joan Larkin, Lorene Lazzar, Jan Heller Levi, Anne Marie Macari, Martin Luther King, Jr. Community Church, Butch Massaro, Paula McLain, Charles Mencel, Tony Medina, E. Ethelbert Miller, Shahari G. Moore, Malena Morling, Roy Nathanson, Alicia Ostriker, Nii Ayikwei Parkes & the UK family, Biela Patricia, Tacuma Roeback, Bruce Smith, Jennifer Steele, Lamont B. Steptoe, Gerald Stern, Becky Thompson, Venus Thrash, Rich Villar, Judith Vollmer, Anne Waldman, Frank X. Walker, Douglas Turner Ward, Michael Waters, Natalie Weikart, the Funky Cold U Street family, and my Contoocook River jumping New England College clan.

Contents

Around the Way

Road Songs

Around the Way

A Nightmare on U Street

I am walking

into Chocolate City

and wondering

why it is still called

by that name.

There are no black

people who live

here. At the New

York Avenue

Gate, I am stopped

by a policemen

with a Doberman.

One of them

speaks to me, and

asks to see my

pass book. I tell

him I live in the

Prince Georges

County Bantustan.

He spits and says

I don't care where

you live Nigger, just

as long as it isn't

near me. When he

calls me outside of

my name, I bite

off his nose

and his ears, and

his tail. Then

I wake up with the

taste of blood

in my mouth, and no

matter what I do

I cannot get it out.

Zero Degrees in Dupont Circle

(4 McKenna's Wagon)

It is the kind of evening when the temperature
sign on the Sun Trust Bank building just says
"Damn it's Cold," the kind of evening where
wind turns tears to hail, and water mains spit up

glaciers; the kind of DC evening where the march
of penguins is the march of pedestrians;
where squirrels wear scarves, and P Street is
an ice road with taxis for truckers; the kind

of hypothermic night where homeless birds
would steal to cop some extra feathers, or do
they covet blankets, or are they really birds
at all, or men who simply look like birds—

or me, flocking to this circle, perching
on these benches, flying from the shadows
to the food truck.

Homeless

Whenever the Cardboard Man
has food, the pigeons have food.
        His fingers are bread crumbs
        for faithful nodding beaks.
                He is their tattered chief
                their perforated commander

who sleeps in a shopping cart
barracks with faded fatigues and a
        donation cup, both in summer
        and in fall—but last night he was
                wounded by the winter. Wind
                chills stymied steam coughing up

to cover his grate. In the wee
hours of the morning, his face grew
        hard like frozen rain. And he
        dreamed a final dream, far from jungles
                and tunnels and pink mist flying from
                the backs of heads. Motionless, he was

when paramedics found him, right
across from Domino's Pizza (where they
        have a special every day), he lay
        with one hand open, almost like he was feeding
                the birds—and the birds all gathered
                round him, almost like they were eating

        an invisible supper.

Dreamgirl

A zaftig sister with Ipod ears and a dandelion
dress sings while waiting for the 90 bus
to Congressional Heights as Duke Ellington
hums along from the front porch

of his mural here above the Green Line
Metro. Her hair is a velvet lounge
of black—waves pulled back
into an obedient teacher's bun, shining

under the follow spot sun like the vinyl
eye of an old school LP, or Armor All on
the tires of a maubi colored Escalade
now double-parked and being towed

in front of Ben's Chili Bowl by one of DC's
finest. At 100 degrees Fahrenheit, humidity
is thicker than grease on chitlins—still
this sister blows—sings like

every stranger passing by is an American
Idol judge—sings as if this urine baked
sidewalk, freckled with its flattened
wads of gum, and crumpled up

McDonald's bags is the polished
stage of the Apollo—sings as if

Carnegie Hall is calling her
name and she knows

the garbage that surrounds
her, will never be
her home.

New York Avenue

(after Thomas Sayers Ellis)

There are no tumble weeds on this road —
        tumble strip clubs
hub caps, cigarettes maybe
     but no weeds.
With concrete hands, asphalt fingers
       the city holds on
       to its own.
Old tires stick
     in hair of bushes
like super-sized licorice lifesavers.
       Traffic lights signal like ushers
     guiding cars into lanes
       like pews.
Spitting distance from sidewalks
       track marks of trains
     are raised on snowy embankments.
It is a high cholesterol street.
     It is a sniper crawl
       shivery morning.
Hawk can see his breath today
     coughing clouds
       into rush-hour sky.
As I watch all the cars passing by me
     tremble-sipping
     from a hot cup of coffee
I cannot help but think of you —
     for
     all their headlights look alike
all their sighs and wipers
     all their honks and whoring
all their high beams, all their heaters

all their headlights
look alike
as only the go go postered trees
bear witness,
standing here beside me
under a revival tent of gray
lifting up their branches
like holy hands.

Ed-ZOO-cation

Seven Benjamin steps down from the big bronze lion
down beyond the Emu with the Slinky in her neck, who
pecks out eyes of fences, down past the Panda Café, the Panda
Pavilion, past the Panda kites—past the Panda cookies
Panda Pampers, and baby wipes—past the Panda produce
Panda onions, past the peas—past the Panda condoms
Panda lip gloss, Panda whiskey—past the Panda Pine-Sol
Panda pies, and Panda cakes—past seven in the Panda pool
hall, and Panda Preparation H, deep in the bamboo hair
of the Asia Trail, about twenty blocks up from Georgetown ER
and a hospital room with a view, a friend of the National Zoo
jumped in the Panda habitat yelling, *Freedom for Big Cuddly!*
Freedom for the black and white! yelling, *Freedom for...oh my*
God he's on me! yelling, *Shoot him, I'm being attacked!* As
shrieks startled sparrows from elephant's backs and gold from
the coats of the lions, and giraffes (who are normally not all
that talkative) were heard to say, *Oh shit!* How unfettered by
wails and moans of men were clouds, and if any saw the pupils
of the sky blink, it never made the news, but no cameras went
home hungry, and no paramedics rushed in to meddle, as every
question about the bite of a Panda with a business plan was settled.

After a White Man Stepped on His Shoes
On K Street, Big Mike Became Completely Visible

Coughing up caps to cotton—parting   the red sea sidewalk. He wa
inconsolable
over
aggravated
Gators
inconsolable
over
violated
bunions
inconsolable
Coughing up caps to cotton—parting   the red sea sidewalk. He
was.

BET

Watermelon glazed fried chicken
     fills our screens.
Pimps on parade tattoo "Bitches"
     on sisters.
DJ Overseer & MC Whipping Post
     play—Buckwheat
Hip Hop, zip-a-dee-doo-dah
     night & day.
Bishop Money's undies—anointed
     & for purchase.
Bootie Entertainment Television
     of thee I sing.
Bootie Entertainment Network—
     no ideas
     but in bling.

The Kool Aid Word

NIGGA! NIGGA!
     NIGGA! NIGGA!
NIGGA! NIGGA!
     NIGGA!

don't you know
     there is nothing
     wrong with the word nigga
     sista?

my mother, my brother don't you know?
     you are my nigga—
     fa shigga

everybody says so—

it's just a word nigga
     jump and dance and sing
     and say it—SAY IT LOUD!

NIGGA! NIGGA!
     NIGGA! NIGGA!
NIGGA! NIGGA!
     NIGGA!

ain't nothing wrong with the word
     or the kool-aid nigga
     take a sip and
     SAY IT!

don't you know there is nothing wrong
with the word
        nothing nothing nothing
wrong with word
                nigga nigga nigga
nigga, bitch, ho—nigga nigga nigga—
nigga yo ho reng ge kyo

NOTHING WRONG   WITH THE WORD

        until

it spills from the mouth
        of a stranger
        and you finally get a chance

        to hear it.

Ode to a Mosquito in Georgetown

Your flutter hovered round my ears—a tiny siren.
You bugged me, but at least you were committed.

There was no neutral in your gears—nothing lazy
in your tongue. And for that, I'm almost

saddened at your passing. But who
are we kidding?

You were born a bloodsucker
and I was born

with lightening
in my hands.

Ode to Caffeine

(4 Mocha Hut, 1301 U Street, NW)

There are days when I would
snort you if I could,

rub chocolate in my skin like
liniment for workweeks.

*Monday Monday, can't trust
that day*—but doppio

espresso, your sip is always
daybreak in a swallow.

A Time to Kiss

Under
the sun
I scuffed
my spirit,
ran my
soul over
chasing after
the wind—a
camera blink
of fame,
a thimble
sip
of power—a
dinghy wake
of bliss,
an entourage
of parrots.
And how
much wine
was wisdom?
And what
good
came
of it?
Until your
lips, nothing.
At least
nothing I
recall, after

guava jelly
kisses, and
fingertips
like whispers.

Homecoming

The crevasse opens.
One lucky climber falls in.
Tonight she says yes.

A Different Kind of Pledge

(4 Cherry & Francis Bellamy)

I pledge allegiance to the flag of the United States of America
and to the Republic for which it stands, one Nation under God,
indivisible, with liberty and justice for all...

Oh hell no, I do not.

I pledge allegiance to the fingers, reading goosebumps
On your breasts like Braille, and to lips steaming hips
Like Tito Puente steaming timbales.

I pledge allegiance to the second mouthpiece, to slowly
Warming up the embouchure, and to sweat as salty
As salsa that falls from your nipples to anoint...

One black man, under Goddess
With multiple orgasms
For all.

June Bugs

Back in the day:

We walked the same way (up Wayne Avenue)
Passed the same deli (Ertter's Market)
At the same time (after school on Thursdays)
Ate at the same restaurant (Eat & Drink)
Ordered the same food (two steak & cheese subs)
Joked with the same cook (Alex Alexandros)
Rode the same bus (the 70 into DC)
Spoke to the same driver (Mr. Johnson, who had a lisp)
Got off at the same stop (right across the District line)
Giggled through the same lobby (The Georgian Inn)
Paid the same clerk (Mr. Patel—$20.00 for a single)
Signed the same names (Mr. & Mrs. Smith from Alaska)
And could hardly holster our laughter, in the lobby
In the elevator, in the room... Because at sixteen
We didn't know that everybody in the world knew

Exactly what we were doing.

Little Ghetto Boy

(4 Donny Hathaway)

1973—Evening under the apple hat sky—fifty rows back at the Carter Baron—You are my heaven—I believe you—My sack full of dreams from 88 pillows—I believe you—A tenor genie—I believe you—A Fender Rhodes Houdini—I believe you—Carpet riding on your Leslie-like vibrato—I believe you—Lifted by your Chicago/DC Soul—I believe you—Carrying me, saying I'm not heavy—I believe you—Carrying us, saying none of your brothers are heavy—I believe you—Singing someday we'll all be free—I believe you—Singing every song like it's your last—I believe you—When you know where love is or when you have to ask—I believe you—Stirring butter with Roberta—I believe you—Saying I can be real black and hang on to the world at the same time—Dammit, I believe you—And even though they found you on the sidewalk fifteen floors below your hotel window, Donnie, this little ghetto boy still believes you.

Grown Now

Never again will I compare you to
          a biscuit
(as much as I like biscuits)or a
          summer's day
of biscuits, fluffy and brown, that
          flake and
fall from lips like petals from lilies
          or a brick
house, or cakes baked in brick houses
          or a cross
bun (although they are to die for)or
          plantains
so tender they melt on teeth of forks
          or Krispy
Kreme donuts, whether honey dipped
          or plain
or mango bottomed apples, or peachy
          bottomed
pears—not that I've lost my love of
          carbohydrates—
or this rain dance of sprinkles on the
          ones and twos
of your breasts—no, it's just I finally
          see you
and have come to understand, there
          has always
been a difference between buttermilk
          and
          being.

Cherry

Cuts eyes and melts steel.
Ripens smiles and orchards dance.
Mother of my child.

The Power of a Teenage Brain

(after Ross Gay)

One year and a day past twelve
        my son turns to me and says

he now has a "teenage brain," and
        that his teenage brain is "banging"

and nothing like the Clearasil brain
        that came before, or the one that

wore a tub of cologne, to try to
        impress the girls. No, he assures me

his teenage brain will "pretty much"
        take his adolescent body to a whole

new level of cool, and as he steps
        out of the bathroom (after an hour)

to break this news—pants lower
        than tiles in the basement—shades

slicker than Diddy's, to humble the
        sun, with toilet paper stuck to

the bottom of his Aqua Jordans—
        all I can do is nod, in agreement.

Sessin for My Son

Soweto rides with us now — this child no longer child —
two parts high school:three parts pimples, with 100 dread
locks coming, who knows that life doesn't add up evenly —
that all life doesn't add up evenly — not like The Count
on Sesame Street once promised it would, or should.
He knows that wars get waged, and soldiers explode on

mines like water balloons — that bullets peck flesh on
people like birds peck earth for worms — that children
find rape in beds, machetes in their heads, and should
this happen to him, whether in Darfur or any dreaded
space, no Batman, or Superman, or Flash, can he count
on to Green-Lantern him back together, nice and even

like before. He also knows, from out-of-gas evenings
and milkless mornings, when money thins like skin on
drums, that parents can war. Too many times to count
he has witnessed his grown ups acting more childish
than children — more hell than holiness — more dread
than alive, fighting in front of him when we shouldn't

have — and not forgiving fast enough when we should.
Tonight, with us he rides, belted in acrimony — but even
with cursing after a six-o-clock churching, our dreadful
Sunday sundown drowning shouts, he won't cry now, on
this his teen titan stage. He will not cry like the child
once did, because I have taught him that tears count

on scales that measure men much like air balls count
in basketball. And he carries this lesson I shouldn't

have preached like a bad tattoo. So, like most man children
he now sits brooding in a stew of silence. And even
as we fight, I feel guilty. Remembering Greenbelt Park on
his birthday—at two—when he chased birds until they dreaded

his pigeon stalker, park sparkler smiles, and how we dreaded
him falling down for the freedom of his tears, countless
as they sometimes were. And I think of the day he threw up on
the barber (after more monsoon weeping), and how I should
have told Mayfield it was his first hair cut that evening
or apologized longer, but then, Mr. Mayfield has children—

all grown—poker faced trees, as Soweto soon will be (that is, should
I blink, or turn away) and I miss my emancipated baby this evening
like I miss the times we knew better than to fight, in front of our child

Begin With God

(after Yehuda Amichai)

Begin with God and end with God. This is the best way to live.
  Before I see yachts docked on the Potomac in Washington Harbor

with barbecue grills growing from their sterns, steaks sizzling
  smoke rings that tickle the chinny chin chins of clouds, feather breezes

rocking bows, in the cradle of late July, swordfish antennas
  topless and flashing over velvet carpet waves, in the shadow

of bistros where couples in bikinis toast to whatever couples in
  bikinis toast to, clinking glasses filled with pearls, here beside

caramel skinned condominiums with trees growing from their
  crowns, and windows that look like they've been polished with

thousand dollar bills—before I see yachts docked on the Potomac,
  Amichai's words are easy to say. After the marina, to utter these words

I must focus like a hunter aiming at a charging lion. There is only
  one bullet left in my gun. *Begin with God and end with…end with…*
                                                             something…

Roxanne's First Law

(4 Sir Isaac Newton & West Virginia Avenue, NE)

Roxanne roulettes
down beer bottle blocks

round crack alley screams
on the ho stroll like

the bug can't catch her
if she's moving.

Visiting Hours are Over

Washington, D.C., has the highest rate of AIDS in the United States, and more babies are born with the AIDS virus in Washington than in other U.S. cities… Of the 12,428 people infected with HIV in Washington, 80 percent are black… Nov 27, 2007 (Reuters) MAGGIE FOX

There are no gay, straight, down low, get high, protected, unprotected sex questions for you now. Now, a morphine drip drains its indifferent bladder in your arm. Now a monitor's beeps get sleepy in the shadow of your coughs. So many came to see you today. So many came and left—although you will not remember: the priest (the only one who touched you), the nurse (who belched as she watched Wheel of Fortune and slurped your soup and juice). I wonder if they knew, you only had one boyfriend (Solomon, in high school, who told you that he loved you. Solomon in high school, who messed with college girls). Well, it doesn't matter now. You are only soiled sheets here, bowing to a full-blown god. The only points to make are hypodermic. Visiting hours are over, but I am here. I am nothing, if not faithful.

Hey Hey Hey

A drunk man with piss for pants is cursing out a Stop sign in July. He wears a brown wool sweater that may once have been a white wool sweater. His face is a canyon of scars—his hair, a snow cap dusting over wrinkled chestnut skin. He accuses the Stop sign of trying to emasculate him and says, *Oh no no no, you WILL listen to what I have to say! Don't you know I will kill you? That's right. Who's afraid now? Look at you now, face all red. How does it feel to be afraid? Huh? Answer me! How does it feel? Don't be standing there all quiet now. You weren't quiet all them years ago when you called me in your office now were you? And when I told you I had three babies, and how I needed that job, how it was only me left, yeah, you had a lot to say then. Couldn't even look me in the eye though, could you? Come talking bout 'Mr. Johnson ain't a team player this and Mr. Johnson, I'm sorry it didn't work out that.' You sorry? YOU sorry? Hey-Hey-Hey, look at me when I'm talking to you! Don't you know everybody gone now? My life's gone now. No, I guess you don't know. Don't care either. But that's alright, un huh, that's perfectly alright, cause I got two team players balled up for you right here, right now bitch! That's right, I said it. I'm the one in charge now, and you can't stop me. Nobody can stop me. The Yield sign can't stop me. The No Trespassing sign can't stop me. And didn't I tell you to stop staring at me? You with your shiny bama shirt on, come looking like one of the Isley Brothers. I'm a man dammit! YOU HEAR ME? A MAN!* He then begins to dance around the Stop sign like Ali circling Liston in '64, bobbing and weaving, toes floating, jabs juking, just two blocks down from the 9:30 Club, where six white college kids are sacking out for tickets to see Mos Def, at one o'clock in the afternoon, melting like fatback in a skillet. Although Pops is stabbing the air with punches—scoring at will, these prospective concert goers barely notice, turning their slight chuckles into yawns and Washington City Papers into fans. As the old man sticks and moves, rope-a-dopes and rages, he suddenly notices a doorway-sized poster pasted on the Vermont Avenue building behind him, and stops. The sign says "Bill Cosby Is Coming to Speak" and that "Black People Should Not Blame White People For Their Problems." Halted by the Cos's premium glossy smile, he slowly crosses the sidewalk, moving like the world is an earthquake that only he can feel, leaning in to read the poster so closely he makes the paper wet with his breath—then his vomit—then, his tears.

Road Songs

Wedding Mourning

(4 Nicole Paultre-Bell & Queens, NY)

The apostles live in Coltrane's horn, they
say, and if you listen closely you can
almost hear them singing their hymns the way
old folks do in church, their hands on his hands
their angel fingers pressing keys for sounds
that some might take for the voice of his sax—
but there's a spirit more than metal bound
to "A Love Supreme," my favorite thing, that
sometimes looks inanimate but lives, like
grass under snow in winter, or bloodroots
in sand waiting for rain, or even like
addicts locked down to make their habits mute—
or me locked in this room behind grief's gate.
When Sean Bell was shot, I heard how God plays.

Miranda Rights for Black Men

You have the right to remain silent, the right to bleed
out, the right to be a cripple after they beat you.

Anything you say can and will be used against you in a court
of law (where they will be acquitted) after they beat you.

Whether in New York or Philly, you have the right to speak
to an attorney, if you can still speak after the beat you.

And to have a lawyer present during questioning is also your right,
but your attorney may be helping them to beat you.

If you cannot afford a lawyer, one will be provided for you,
which may be worse than letting somebody beat you.

If you decide to answer questions without an attorney
present, you can stop—no one's listening when they beat you.

Do you understand these rights as I have read them to you?
Nod for yes, if you can breathe after they beat you.

On Wallets Mistaken for Pistols and Forgiveness

I would turn the other cheek, but there is a bullet hole there
    America
    jacuzzi
    for
    hatred
    America
    wheelchair
    for
    justice
    America
I would turn the other cheek, but there is a bullet hole there

Taller

Work bound with
the forgotten. They
like moles, in gritty
like cribs—los niños
underground. As we
of the R Train, hard
to Chamber Street
our faces soon to be
sauce from the day,
towers. *Son, when*
don't care how long
as it's taller, I'll be
with sinkhole eyes
in and says, *Yeah*
and can you help
cents? We both say
Right, like I was
we bounce some
clouds this time.
Oprah money, but
Right? Can't let
your house piss
Can't let some
your woman while
beside you warming
gotta show them
this country is all
Am I right? I mean
kick the hell out

Pops, we pass
sleep in tunnels
grimy crannies
invisibles—
ride in the belly
hats, headed in
from Bay Ridge,
sunburned, like red
my father talks
we build it back,
it takes. As long
happy. A lady
who listens, leans
baby, size matters,
me out   with fifty
no. He continues,
saying, I hope
steel off the
Might cost that
it's worth it.
nobody come in
in yo sugar boy.
towel head smack
she right there
up the bed. We
Al-Qaida what
about. Am I right?
Iraq, Iran, whoever—
all them jokers,

I say. Stomp 'em
what I say. Why
hate in 'em anyway?
heard about
ghost planes, or
the Abu Ghirab
news. He says no,
he doesn't like to talk

back to sand, that's
folks got so much
I ask him if he's
Guantanamo or
if he ever saw
post cards in the
and he whispers
politics on the train.

Dog Tossing

(after Tony Medina)

They say
a Labrador Retriever
is a bird dog.

From
a blood brick
tenement rooftop

some children
put the theory
to the test.

In the soul
dipped village of
Harlem

you have to prove
everything.

The Chronicles of SueKeithia

Dear Diary,

My sixth grade report is going to be on Mr. Hugo Chavez and Mr. Tupac Shakur since the teacher said we had to write about something happening in New Jersey. The newsman said that Mr. Hugo wants to give poor folks some oil and Mr. Tupac is going to help him out by putting him in one of his raps. The man said that the President is mad about it too and calling them names and stuff. I don't understand why everybody fighting. If Mr. Hugo wanted to give me some oil, I would say thank you. A lot of times my mother asks me to put some oil in my hair and we don't have any. That gets on my nerves cause it's not even my fault we run out. My sister with her big head self always be taking more than she need and it's not just me who says she has a big head. Leroy on the 9th floor says she has a big head. Nikki on the 12th floor says she has a big head. She say my sister have a big mouth too, but I know it ain't no bigger than hers cause when she saw me kiss Leroy in the hallway that time she went and told everybody at school, everybody in the building, everybody in Newark seem like, in just one night. She made me so mad I started to pop her in her big mouth, but I didn't cause she really my friend and most the time she be looking out for me when I'm on the playground. You need friends on the playground. I think Mr. Tupac knows that. He has a nice smile. I think if he was my friend nothing bad would ever happen to me. Anyway, I don't know if the President right to be so mad over some hair grease. Even if it's good hair grease. But if you ask me, if somebody act like they want to give you something, and you need it, you should try not to be too mean to them.

Suke 9/28/2006   *

What SueKeithia Wrote about the Black Arts Movement

Dear Diary,

Today in school, Mr. Kazloftsky told us about the Black Arts Movement. I learned all about a man called Amiri Baraka who changed his name from Leroy. If my name was Leroy, I would change it too. He reminds me of my Uncle Bubba who plays the saxophone all the time. Uncle Bubba went to Africa and when he came back, he changed his name to Brother Saalim Salaam. It's hard for me to say his new name cause every time I stutter, so mostly I just hug him and smile. I hope he don't get too mad at me. I wish I could talk like Mr. Kazloftsky. Mr. Kazloftsky loves a poet named Nikki and somebody named Gwendolyn too. I like their pictures. They are pretty ladies. They look like they don't have any trouble talking. They look like they could write a story so good it would make you want to change your name. When I asked Mr. Kazloftsky what happened to the Black Arts Movement, he said it was over. He said it stopped in 1975 exactly. I wonder how he knew that. Anyway, it made me sad that it was over, so I'm going to start it up again. I'm calling all my friends in the building and even my big head sister, and we're going to write our pencils down to the nubs. When I asked Mr. Kazloftsky if the White Arts Movement stopped, he just coughed and looked at me funny. He didn't say anything to me after that.

Suke 10/01/2006

SueKeithia on the Color Red

Dear Diary,

My cousin Lisa got hit by a car last week. She was only six years old and was crossing the street to go to the playground. I have cried all the tissue paper up and cried all the toilet paper too. My sister is doing even worse than me, and Mama says we both are going to need to talk to somebody like Dr. Phil. But I don't know Dr. Phil, and I don't want to talk to anybody. Some of the older boys always be flying down the street, always be playing their music loud and rapping instead of paying attention. Everybody think they the next Biggie. Everybody wanna be like Jay-Z and them. But Jay Z probably know better than to be driving so fast. And if he did hit somebody I don't think he would ever try to run away. Anyway, that's what happened. Some boy was rapping when he should have been driving. We went to the funeral at New Hope Baptist church, and the Deacons who were praying kept talking about God making a way out of no way, and God causing blind men to see. But I don't know what that has got to do with Lisa. I mean, everybody know that Lisa wasn't blind, and even if she was, blind people can see lots of things. Mr. Johnson who lives on the 17th floor is blind and everyday since my cousin got dragged he sits in the lobby saying "red, red, red." He wasn't even there but I can tell he saw exactly what happened. And Lisa didn't need God to make a way out of no way. What she needed was for God to make her a stop sign and some speed bumps and a cross walk.

Suke 2/26/2007

Park Heights Avenue

(4 Charm City)

On my walk to school past Super Kennedy Fried Chicken
and Island Grill, where one time I found a roach leg in my

beef patty, I see houses boarded with steps like broken gray
teeth, windows shut like plywood eyes. Daddy says things

crumble not from being stepped on, but from being forgotten.
I count 3 police cars, 3 condoms, 3 needles, corner to corner.

There are 3 churches: 1 Catholic, 1 Baptist, 1 AME. They
all have nice steps. Once I asked Daddy why we couldn't

have remembered steps, like churches. He just shook his
head and said 13-year-old girls shouldn't question God.

A block down from the blue-blink cameras, Miss Mary has
her palm reading parlor. It used to be a barbershop, then

a record store, then a nail salon, before Mr. Kim got shot.
Springtime, boys on stoops holla, but I don't hear them

On my walk to school, all I hear is Daddy's voice going
off like a siren in my head saying, *Dogs can sweet talk*

Baby, and how he doesn't want to have to kill anybody
unless he has to.

Oh Baltimore

B'more, white steps, black man, war chiseled canyons
under raven eyes, mustache and goatee frost riding rusted
skin, stoop sentinel for grandsons bouncing wisdom knees
in summer, sits undefeated by Cain, left hand clenching cola
right hand sunning scars; could split brick, baffle bullets with a
stare—and has, he will tell you, survived both Vietnam and Ameri

I Love it When You Call Me Big Country

(4 Asha & Affrilachia)

I'm on my way down home
wondering what draws me back

almost cicada-like, from cocoa Santa land
to Lynchaniggah City.

Hills scraped by dynamite fingers
watch the road, lifting me to Mammoth–

12 miles from the K-Mart in Glasgow
a million miles from black hair care products.

Then, flipping digits, I hear it.
On 99.1 FM, Sentimental Sunday

Johnny walks the line, Loretta answers
daughter of coal mine.

Dolly says she'll always love me
& both Whitney & I understand.

Blue grass got in my locks
before Biggie did.

Imagine

(after the Ninth Ward & John Lennon)

Imagine we've forgotten
It's easy if you try
The ghost of death abiding
In post-Katrina eyes
Imagine all the people
Drowning in their dreams...

Imagine unemployment
It isn't hard to do
A shanty town of trailers
The families with no food
Imagine all the people
Sinking in their screams...

You may say I'm a dreamer
But I'm not the only one
Oiling suicide in pistols
Wading nightmares in the sun

Imagine poor possessions
Paved over in the ground
A Starbucks in the 9th Ward
The bodies never found
Imagine all the people
Gated off and lost...

You may say I'm a dreamer
But I'm not the only one
Loading suicide in pistols
Wading nightmares in the sun

Blind Horse

Emery is a blind horse now
and I don't know how to lead him.
There is nothing wrong with his eyes
but he hugs the walls when he walks—at
      San Antonio Elementary, and in
        this roach motel apartment. Two years
         after bubbles filled with screams, he is
          bruises born of doorknobs, stumble food for
          chairs—corralled down in first grade, when he
        should be up in third. Two years after water rose like
       stopped up toilets, and we saw you slip off of our Jezebel
      roof, he wakes up shouting, Don't let me fall! Don't let me
     sink! Don't let me fall! And I don't know how to help him
    Mama, cause even though I'm eighteen, I'm tied to my own
   whimpers, and everyday I jump and bump and bruise myself,
when I hear a faucet run, when I feel a raindrop.

Arrest Me

Old South...Jena...the white man who pulled the shotgun at the convenience store wasn't charged with any crime at all. But the three black youths in that incident were arrested and accused of aggravated battery and theft after they wrestled the weapon from the man... JENA, Louisiana May 20, 2007 (Chicago Tribune) HOWARD WITT

If grabbing the gun from a man about to shoot me is thievery
then go ahead, double barrel arrest me—arrest me now.

If grabbing the gun from a man about to shoot me is robbery
then go ahead, double barrel address me—capture me now—
steel bracelet snap me. Do quickly what you are going to do.

If aiming a gun at a sheet about to shoot me is felony, go ahead
then, double barrel back me—steel bracelet smack me. Arrest
me now—right now. Whatever you are going to do—quickly
do, and cut me off. You know about cutting off, don't you?

If beating the man with the gun about to shoot me is savagery
then go head on, cold cock kick me—steel toe tap me, and call
for back up now. Quickly, do what you are going to do—cut me
and mine off, like you always wanted to and don't hold back, cut
off the circulation in my wrists like you been practicing—laugh.

If snatching the gun from the punk ass man about to shoot me
is larceny then go on ahead, steel bar stain me—toilet chain me—
call your back up's back up, quickly quickly do whatever it is
you are going to. Cut off, cut off, you know, the circulation in
my wrists, just like you practised practised, until my veins
swell up like hot air balloons and pop up, pop up—burst.

Charge me with felonious self-respect and wash your hands.
Say the people called me king (or that I tried to run for president).
Impeach me for displaying alarming, and gratuitous sanity.
Prosecute me for reckless and premeditated self-defense. Put me
on trial for wanton and public disregard of white supremacy,
and I will not resist, for in this regard I am guilty, and as long
as I live, I will be.

Upon Waking Up Black in Henniker, New Hampshire

(4 Judith Vollmer)

1.
I wake up in a New England motel room.
I have come to get lost in poetry. It is too
early to look for a compass. I have separation

anxiety from my mattress. I look for my cell phone
to see what time it is. I look for my cell phone
because the battery in my watch has died.

Everything dies—but you knew that. It's 6:52 AM
according to the phone. I climb back into bed.
I have anxiety from my mattress—

separation. I tell myself there is still more time
for sleep. I am lying to myself. Everybody
lies, but then again, you knew that.

Green of spring glows through my window.
The sky is an ocean with clouds as sailing
ships. My toes kiss the cool of the

blue gray speckled floor. My arms hug clothes
that hang on the edge of clean. I sniff and
sniff and sniff. I am decidedly funky

but not irreparably so. I zombie-walk to the bathroom
to shower and answer the call. I carry along
the essentials: towel, toothpaste, soap

washcloth, mirror, shaver. Water on: I edify
all my most valuable players. Water off:
I drip and dab and dash.

2.
I remember flying into Manchester Airport and
thinking New Hampshire looked like a
giant green afro from the sky, and I

loved this airborne vision—trees that look like no
one was ever lynched from them—or whipped
or burned, or cut. Though I know this isn't

true, when I walk through Henniker's hurryless
hillsides, it feels like I'm massaging
the overburdened temples of the earth.

3.
How is it possible I will forget the pleasure of
this day? You know I will. Everything
you know. Still I wish it were

possible to hold on. I wonder: why is it
that no one ever suffers from post
traumatic happiness? Or ever

flashes back to unbearable joy and has to
seek immediate treatment? Today two
white men in a truck with gun racks

stopped so I could cross the street—almost
as if it wasn't the law—almost as if
they didn't have to, and no

nooses hung from tailgates. No one
had to be dredged up from the
bottom of the river.

They smiled until I smiled. They waved until
I waved. It is 11:00 PM on a Wednesday—
yes, I would like to remember this day.

Peace Be Still

Believe

It begins in Odenton—here on the Penn Line train with orange and black Cal Ripken, Jr. jerseys. Though he hasn't played for years, his streak suits up for every game. It lives on the backs of these ten year olds who squeeze into their seats and reach up to palm read windows. Every one of them will catch a homerun ball tonight—every one, they say, as they board the car with mitts under arms. They are pining for the Yard—pining for the shine of its big black metal gates—drawn like chicks in spring to chirping. And so we ride, after what seems to me forever, until our commuter car finally reaches the ball park. When the train peels back its sardine can doors, we spill out and file by the wrong handed Babe Ruth statue on Eutaw Street (file by grilled panini sandwiches, old fashioned hand dipped ice cream, Cracker Jacks and pretzels, souvenir soda and beer) to splash our bottoms down on every fold out seat of the stadium. Vendors pitch peanuts like fastballs, running up and down steps, lining lemonade in trays wider than the outfield. When the National Anthem is sung, the "Oh" in "Oh say can you see," is replaced by an O for Orioles in a stadium wide shout. I am surprised by this. Baltimore is not. They believe, and have already seen miracles—2,131 of them. So it really doesn't matter that the food costs twice as much as air. No, it really doesn't matter that the Birds haven't won a series since 1983—or that the Rangers beat them 10 to 1 last night. Charm gate fans are faithful. I on the other hand, believe in hand offs, end zones, excitement. There hasn't been much of that tonight.

After seven scoreless innings, the only action has come from a
child of Satan's spawn, who kicks at my seat from behind, and
from a baby to my right with Pavarotti's lungs, and an outhouse
in his Pampers. It is hot. My mouth is a dune. I am ready to go.
But, just as I stand in the stretch, to sprint my way to the exit, I
hear the crack of a bat and turn, and despite myself I see it. Then
I, even I, who said he hated baseball, I who floated in on the back
of a friend's free ticket (and even then complained), cannot help
but jump over two rows of terrace seats, three bags of popcorn
with butter, four slices of pizza with sausage and pepperoni, to
catch a foul ball on a Saturday evening, and curl my fingers into
smiles.

What Pastor Said

(after Rev. Darrell S Greene)

I have been told
after Easter service ends
and benediction's organ
lifts resurrection praise
to Zion's gates

in the prayer polished air
of the lower auditorium
a savory, southern
soulful meal will be served.

Now, the doctor
in the house
has told us to stay away
from fried chicken

but I had to remind the doctor;
we are black
and it is Sunday.

How I Learned Not to Play in Church

(4 Mrs. Velaine E. Macklin)

Mother hit me with her eyes from the choir loft: playing in church
can get you killed.
Sharpshooter:
crosshairs
for
eyelashes
Sharpshooter:
Annie
Oakley
alto
Sharpshooter:
Mother hit me with her eyes from the choir loft: playing in church
can get you killed.

O2B Ushers

Who but Motown soldiers move like Baptist ushers
marching seams and creases, up Easter isles. Flower
hats nod, fluttering fans smile, confirming these men,
the coolest alive. Oh Mary watch the feet! Tell Martha
Steps this sweet are worthy of tears, and moaning
is good. Dap begins the dance, glove to white glove
black suit to back pew, as salted pepper fros settle newly
planted cornrows, before Leslies spin processional. Then
as drums cut, a rock of slavery ages struts remixed on
the mirror slippers of its sons. The polish of brotherhood!
Is that David or Deacon Ruffin leading? I cannot tell.
Four little girls, ribbons under bonnets, strain to see—
men, Temptation walking stained glass rainbows
as always, moving forward.

Doonie

comes to practice wrapped in autumn evening, 95 and fly
Butterfinger cheeks and a magnet smile. They say she put
the bounce in B'more, back in Pullman Porter days. Her life
has been to music what sugar is to glaze. Once, her voice
could blush the blue jays into cardinals. Her fingers, still stride
ragtime over hymns. Out of respect, even the piano squares his
shoulders, when she walks into the room. And tonight, as she
parks her silver cane on the stoic curb of the upright, she says
we should prepare to sing a very solemn song. And tonight
as we bind our hands like breathing vines, bow our heads
close our eyes, she turns to the choir and says, *You know,*
I could kill a pork chop right about now. And right about then
we are no more good for the singing, of very solemn songs.

A Day of Presence

After coffles marching sorrow
After sixty million sold
After screams crossing spoonways in faeces & blood

After dysentery waves
After eight week nights
After Small Pox shackles over keloid seas

After shark chum babies
After gang tackle rape
After anchors dropping terror & auction block parades

After King Cotton reveille
And twenty hour fear
After dirt floor pillows & maggot pork buffets

After runaway castration
And freedom's severed ears
After tears for irrigation & broken teeth for seeds

After frostbite shanties
And crushing heat in cane
After hogshead nail rolls & souls as backhoes

After Dred Scott ushered
And Lincoln's crying booth
After black code blisters & 40 acre lies

After Ruby cried rape
And Vicky cried 9
After Scottsboro berries swelling death row vines

After lynch party picnics
And Rosewood human grilles
After Mamie doubled over & Emmett's eye spilled

After Medgar's moaning driveway
After DeLa Beckwith's glee
After kerosene for crosses & Klansmen for police

After shotgun-showered ballrooms
And bombs for little girls
After kings turning cheeks, jaws exploding like grenades

After green miles for Mumia
After Amadou was bled
After fifty rounds for bride grooms & axes in our heads

After After After After
After After After After, After After
After After, After After After After...

We are here, my people
Pa'lante, my people—bruised soles
Upon souls—still here—fire proof, in churches of the heart

Counter punches wrapped
In halting hallelujahs
Traveling mercies prayed over shepherd boy's slings

And nothing can erase us
From this rock where we stand
            for we are rooted, like blood in Canaan land.

Cyrus Chestnut @ the Last Supper Service

Bethany Baptist Church, 4:00 PM, and I am here
for the transubstantiation service—for the body of
Jesus in a wafer—his blood in Welch's Grape juice
and a little plastic cup, and because Cyrus Chestnut
is playing. He sits, black tie, suit, and glasses—not

with Wynton at the Lincoln Center—not at the Jazz
Standard in Manhattan—not with Sister Battle at the
Kennedy Center on the lapping lips of the Potomac
but here in Baltimore, where he always returns to
commune with scales and angels. When the Pastor

calls for the song "Let Us Break Bread Together,"
right after the sermon, every sin in the building falls
on its knees, as Amadeus, Tatum, and Thomas A.
Dorsey seem to enter his fingers. The ease and
unexpected turns of his hover happy hands melt

the keys, causing a man I have never met to nudge me
in the side until my ribs are bruised, saying Oh my
God, oh my God did you hear what he just played?
And I do hear and I am tempted to stand up and shout
Oh hell yes! and Damn, Brother Cyrus can play!

But then, I remember I am still in church and such
exclamations would probably not swallow well during
communion, so I close my eyes because reverence has
sealed them, and because some gifts are so great, it is
better not to look them in the face.

Vacation Bible School

Jordan got a splinter today—big one.

     Kind of splinter that doesn't care if you're Autistic—

doesn't care if you play all by yourself

     or won't let people touch you. And Jordan must

have known that, cause when the wood

     from the swings dug a mine in his finger, he calmly

walked across the playground, said

     excuse me to the other children, and asked me

for some tweezers and a hug.

There is No Fried Chicken in Heaven

(after Gerald Stern)

In all these bank glass pawn shops
in all this wounded hardware
I have never seen a broader bottomed boom box
nor heard Kirk Franklin spin the way I did
at the annual Martin Luther King, Jr. Community Church
picnic, where plates were filled with barbeque and belches
as summer steamed with candied sweets and greens
nor laughed quite as long as I did then—
so hard I thought my heart might explode
from deacons playing the dozens
dancing dominoes in 2006—in Washington, DC
home of Go Go and mosquitoes with a work ethic
as horseshoes fell with thuds like severed tree limbs
my mother's arms all hugs, holding me
like she would never let me go—and playing tag
running like I would die if someone got me—
running like my brother taught me to run—running
like my brother must have run, the day they got him
in that other picnic—that Iraqi picnic
where legs were lost like pennies in the sand
and red was the only color spilling
over punch bowls.

G.I. Joe

By the end of Christmas Day
Joe was nothing more than
torso chasing arms and legs
and head down a Hot Wheels

track. Unprepared for the trauma
that was a ten year-old
president, I pitied him—his
uniform torn like gift wrap

and scattered across the living
room battlefield. I wondered
what recruiters down at Toys
"R" Us said, to talk him

into the box. I wondered if
they promised him college
or a penis, before they shipped
him to the front of the shelf

or if they told him his job
as toilet bowl diver was
for the few, the proud, the brave.

Marley: Wailing for Peace

You are here, one love, from Zig to Zion
marching, filling porridge bowls with "Get up
Stand up" stew, to holler down the liars
and pull up shrubs whose roots are oil and blood.
You are here, one heart, O Jah mighty man,
a steady skanking spear, the toughest gong
still, Les Paul like a plowshare in your hand,
wrecking-ball chants for walls of Babylon—
cancer-free in DJ crates and speakers
without collapse as picket signs make waves.
Play on, unbreakable Trenchtown preacher
from Downing Street doorbells to White House gates.
Redemption songs, your songs of freedom breathe.
Redemption songs, your songs of freedom lead.

We Hope You Enjoyed Reading!
Let us know what you think by sending an e-mail to
books@flippedeye.net

Thank You for buying *A Day of Presence*. If you would like more information about flipped eye publishing, please join our mailing list online at **www.flippedeye.net**.

Visit our other imprints online:

mouthmark *(poetry)*
www.flippedeye.net/mouthmark

lubin & kleyner *(fiction)*
www.flippedeye.net/lubinandkleyner

waterways *(poetry)*
www.waterways-publishing.com

Lightning Source UK Ltd.
Milton Keynes UK
UKHW010719210321
380690UK00001B/36